# The Official Commemorative Book of The United States Olympic Committee

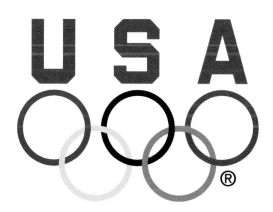

Mike Powell/Allsport

# Let the Games Begin

*Editor/Writer*
**Darcy Steinfeld**

*Feature Writer*
**Douglas S. Looney**

*Designer*
**Cindy Bonds, Gravlee Graphics**

*Publisher*
**Wallace Sears**

*Editorial Assistant*
**David Sears**

*Photography*
**Allsport**
London, New York, Los Angeles,
Sydney, Melbourne
**The Salt Lake Organizing Committee**

*Special Editorial Assistance Provided
by the U.S. Olympic Committee*
*Managing Director for Media & Public Affairs*
**Mike Moran**

*Director of Media Services*
**Bob Condron**

A special thanks to
The U.S. Biathlon Association,
The U.S. Bobsled and Skeleton Federation,
USA Curling, The U.S. Figure Skating
Association, USA Hockey, The U.S. Luge
Association, The U.S. Ski and Snowboard
Association, and U.S. Speed Skating.

RECEIVED
NOV 1 9 2002
BCCC - NIXON

**Pachyderm Press**

P.O. Box 661016 • Birmingham, AL 35266-1016
www.pachydermpress.com

U.S. Olympic Committee, One Olympic Plaza, Colorado
Springs, CO 80909-5760, 719/632-5551

ISBN 1-9316560-4-5

796·48
LET

# Table of Contents

SALT
LAKE
2002

# SALT LAKE 2002

The Olympic flag billows in the strong Canadian wind
at the 1988 Winter Olympic Games in Calgary.
Mike Powell/Allsport

# Salt Lake 2002

by Douglas S. Looney

**Why can't the Salt Lake City Olympic Winter Games start tomorrow?**

**This waiting is excruciating.**

Indeed, the USA – and the rest of the world – is shuffling its skis, clapping its hands, and jumping up and down as everyone looks forward with unbridled enthusiasm to the Games that start February 8, 2002.

No wonder, because we know the brilliantly spectacular environs of Salt Lake City and the oh-so-close Wasatch Range are all set to host a radiant show that will sparkle, shine, glimmer, glisten, and enchant.

We will witness grace and beauty in the ice, snow, and cold. Triumphant moments will be frozen in time. Close your eyes and you can envision possible tableaus that await.

Might figure skater Michelle Kwan, runner-up in Nagano four years ago, end up bedecked in gold in Salt Lake? Easy to picture.

Both the U.S. men and women have excellent chances in ice hockey; short track skater Apolo Anton Ohno, a Seattle teenager, could prosper; ditto American women bobsledders Jean Racine and Jennifer Davidson; men's Super G

Salt Lake City and the Wasatch Range are ready to host the Olympic Winter Games in February 2002.    Brian Bahr/Allsport

SALT
LAKE
2002

competitor Daron Rahlves is a strong contender. Could all end up atop the medal awards podium waving their arms as the Red, White, and Blue flutters on snowy winter nights? Easy to picture.

Who will steal our hearts and put lumps in our throats the way speedskater Dan Jansen did in the '80s and '90s? He was figured to have a decent chance of medaling in either the 500 or 1,000-meter races in 1984. He didn't. Then he was favored to win both in 1988. But he fell in both, competing just after his sister died. He failed in both events again in 1992. In 1994, he failed in the 500 – again – and had only the 1,000-meter left in what was figured to be his final Olympic effort ever.

He won, in world record time. There wasn't a dry eye in the world.

Jansen's name is inscribed on every Perseverance Trophy. So, too, is Salt Lake's.

Consider: Salt Lake was the U.S. candidate for the 1972 Olympic Games, but Sapporo was chosen. It wanted to be the U.S. candidate again for 1976 but Denver was chosen. Subsequently, Denver pulled out and Salt Lake was selected as the replacement U.S. candidate, but Innsbruck was chosen. Salt Lake wanted to be America's choice for both the '92 and '94 Games, but Anchorage was the U.S. pick. Salt Lake was named the U.S. candidate for 1998, but Nagano was chosen.

Six all-out tries to be the host of the Olympic Winter Games; six screaming defeats. This definitely can try a city's spirit.

Happily, what the defeats did was strengthen the resolve of the friendly, helpful, courteous people of Salt Lake. Whenever these good and resilient folks heard the answer was no, they took it as a definite maybe. And redoubled their efforts.

Above: Cathy Turner sheds tears of joy after winning gold for USA in the 500 meter Short-Track Speed Skating event at the '94 Lillehammer Olympic Winter Games.　　　　Shaun Botterill/Allsport

Left: Eric Bergoust rejoices after winning gold in Freestyle Aerials at the 1998 Winter Olympics in Nagano, Japan.
　　　　Nathan Bilow/Allsport

Finally, Salt Lake was chosen as the U.S. candidate for the 2002 Games, and, glory be and hallelujah, The City That Doesn't Know How to Quit was selected by the International Olympic Committee as host.

Do you believe in miracles?

How easy it would have been for Salt Lake City to give up and say phooey on the Olympic Winter Games.

Dan Jansen and Salt Lake City are simpatico.

And all the rest of us get to reap the benefits of Salt Lake's great, good spirit, as the Olympic Winter Games return to American hills and venues for the first time since Lake Placid hosted the Games in 1980.

What a show it will be. The first Winter Games in 1924 attracted 294 competitors from 16

Eric Heiden, the only man to sweep all five Speed Skating Olympic events, will return to the Olympics in 2002 as the team physician for USA Speed Skating.
Tony Duffy/Allsport

Right: Ever the fighter, Austrian Hermann Maier hopes to battle the odds and ski after his motorcycle accident in August 2001.

Todd Warshaw/Allsport

countries in 18 events; Salt Lake will have as many as 2,300 competitors from 80 nations in 70 events.

Remember, it's very slick out there. Athletes most of us have never heard of will zoom to the head of the class; some of the elite will falter. Experience has taught us anything is

Left: Picabo Street proudly displays her Super-G gold medal won in Nagano at the '98 Olympic Winter Games.

Mike Powell/Allsport

possible. Proof? In 1994, the Jamaica bobsled team beat the U.S. Imagine, Jamaican bobsledders?

Let the sliding, gliding, racing, and skating begin – soon – because waiting for this dazzling panoply to unveil itself is agony.

light the
fire within

SALT LAKE 2002

XIX OLYMPIC WINTER GAMES · XIXES JEUX OLYMPIQUES D'HIVER

Team USA celebrates after miraculously beating Finland for the gold medal at the '80 Olympic Winter Games in Lake Placid, NY.

Steve Powell/Allsport

# Winter Olympic History

# Winter Olympic History

Chamonix to Salt Lake City

Top: Frenchman Jean-Claude Killy (left) won all the Alpine events at the 1968 Winter Olympic Games in Grenoble, France.

Allsport Hulton Deutsch/Allsport

Bottom: Sonja Henie, a gold medalist in 1928, 1932 and 1936, is considered one of the greatest figure skaters in history.

IOC Olympic Museum/Allsport

SALT
LAKE
2002

After experiencing freakish weather including, first no snow and then too much, the inaugural Olympic Winter Games began on January 25, 1924 in the little resort town of Chamonix, France. Originally called "International Winter Sports Week," the inaugural Winter Games featured 294 athletes from 16 nations participating in 18 events.

It took 28 years from the start of the Modern Olympics for the Winter Games to emerge, but growing enthusiasm for winter sports finally propelled Bobsleigh, Ice Hockey, Figure Skating, Speed Skating, Cross Country Skiing, Ski Jumping, and Nordic Combined into the international spotlight.

Team USA has seen its share of spectacular wins during the Winter Games. American brothers Jennison and John Heaton won the gold and silver medals in Skeleton at the 1928 Games in St. Moritz. John came back to St. Moritz 20 years later at the ripe-old age of 48 to win the silver medal again when Skeleton was included as a competition sport for the second time.

Dick Button will live forever in Olympic history for winning consecutive gold medals in Figure Skating during the 1948 and 1952 Winter Games.

In 1980, Eric Heiden took home all five gold medals in Speed Skating, the most of any Winter Olympian in a single year. Bonnie "the Blur" Blair achieved the five gold medal status in Speed Skating as well, in 1980, 1992 and 1994.

The United States participated in both the Summer and Winter Games from the very beginning. In fact, the first ever Winter Olympic gold medal presented was won by American Speed Skater Charles Jewtraw in the 500-meter race.

Two U.S. cities have proudly hosted the Winter Games a total of three times. Lake Placid, NY twice in 1932 and 1980, and Squaw Valley, CA once in 1960.

The Figure Skating events at the '32 Lake Placid Games were held indoors for the first time, allowing

Norwegian ice queen Sonja Henie to win her second of three consecutive gold medals in an unprecedented style that would change the sport forever.

The U.S. home team did well in the medal totals category. Eddie Eagan took home his second gold medal as a member of the four-man Bobsled team. With his 1920 gold medal in Boxing, Eagan is the only man ever to win events at both the Summer and Winter Olympic Games. The U.S. won the most medals, 12 overall, which boosted the morale of Depression-era America.

The biggest event at the Squaw Valley Games in 1960 was the surprise win by the U.S. Hockey team. This first U.S. televised Olympic Games also saw comeback gold medal victories by Carol Heiss and David Jenkins, who won silver and bronze for the U.S. in Figure Skating at the '56 Cortina d'Ampezzo Winter Games.

When the Games returned to Lake Placid in 1980, no one thought the U.S. Hockey team would be the top story. When Al Michaels, ABC announcer, exclaimed, "Do you believe in miracles?" the American audience said yes!

The world watched in disbelief as a collection of U.S. college players beat the powerful – and favored – Soviet Union team 4-3, and then beat Finland 4-2 two days later to win the gold medal.

In 2002, Herb Brooks, the '80 "Miracle on Ice" coach, returns as the U.S. head coach and is hoping for another miracle.

This February, Salt Lake City will host the world at the XIXth Olympic Winter Games. Over 2,300 athletes from 80 nations are expected to participate in 70 events in the Salt Lake area. Such athletes as Michelle Kwan, Apolo Anton Ohno, Tricia Byrnes and Alan Alborn hope to be added to the list of such triumphant Olympians as Peggy Fleming, Jean-Claude Killy, Katarina Witt and Dan Jansen.

To list all of the amazing heroes and heroines from the 74 years of Olympic Winter Games history would take up this entire book. But one thing is sure – those watching the 2002 Winter Games will see a new chapter in Olympic history unfolding before their eyes.

Above: Flag bearers representing the 16 nations participating in the first Olympic Winter Games take the Olympic Oath in Chamonix, France in 1924.                                    IOC Olympic Museum/Allsport

Center: A portrait of Pierre de Fredi Baron de Coubartin, the Frenchman who lead the charge to revive the Olympic Games.
                                    IOC/Allsport

Left: American Richard Button, the first to perform a triple loop, won the Figure Skating gold medal in 1948 and 1952.
                                    IOC/Allsport

# Olympic Location Preview

The United States Olympic team passes by Governor Franklin Delano Roosevelt who presided over the '32 Olympic Winter Games in Lake Placid, NY and later watched his wife Eleanor take a ride down the bobsled track.                     Hulton/Allsport

# Olympic Location Preview

A view of Salt Lake City as the moon rises above the Wasatch Mountain Range.

Brian Bahr/Allsport

With an exemplary climate, the majestic Wasatch Mountain Range, and the world's best facilities, Salt Lake City was proud to be chosen as host of the XIXth Olympic Winter Games.

In addition to Salt Lake City, the surrounding towns of Ogden, Provo, Park City, and Heber City along with Park City Mountain Resort, Deer Valley Resort, and Snowbasin Ski Resort have succeeded in a remarkable effort to build, update, and improve facilities to accommodate the 2002 Winter Games in the best way possible.

## Utah and Salt Lake City Facts

Population *(Source – US Census Bureau 2000)*

| | |
|---|---|
| Utah Population | 2,233,169 |
| Salt Lake City Population | 171,151 |
| Greater Salt Lake Area Population | 1,622,073 |

Elevation and Climate *(Source – National Weather Service)*

Salt Lake Elevation 4,330 feet/1,320 meters

Climate *(Average Daily Temperature)*

| | | | | |
|---|---|---|---|---|
| January | 28 F | | April | 50 F |
| February | 34 F | | May | 59 F |
| March | 41 F | | June | 69 F |

Salt Lake City's quest to host the Winter Games began in January of 1966 when it was named as the USA candidate city to host the 1972 Games. Unsuccessful in that bid, Salt Lake City continued to pursue the goal of hosting a Winter Olympic Games.

The road to success began in January 1995, when Salt Lake City was chosen by the International Olympic Committee (IOC) as one of four finalists to host the 2002 Winter Olympic Games. Then, at the 104th IOC Session in June 1995, Salt Lake City was selected to be the host in the first ballot vote.

The state of Utah takes its name from one of the first known tribes to roam the area, the Ute Indian tribe. The first known tribe to reside in the Salt Lake area from A.D. 1 to 1300 was the Pueblo, also known as the Anasazi (Ancient) Indians. The first non-Native American settlers to permanently set up residence in the arid valley were members of the Church of Jesus Christ of Latter-day Saints, led by Brigham Young. Young and his followers entered the Valley of the Great Salt Lake on July 24, 1847 after fleeing religious persecution in Illinois. Young saw the valley and declared, "This is the right place. Drive on." Only 148 people, including just three women and two children, trudged into what would later be known as Salt Lake City.

Today, the population of Utah is over two million and growing. The majority of people live in Salt Lake, Weber, Utah, and Davis Counties.

The city of Salt Lake is situated on land that used to be covered by Lake Bonneville. This prehistoric lake later dissipated into what is now the Great Salt Lake, the second-largest saltwater lake in the world. Surrounding the city is the Wasatch Range of the Rocky Mountains to the east and the Oquirrh Mountains to the west. Those events not held in the cities of Ogden, Provo and Salt Lake City will be in smaller towns and resorts within the Wasatch Range.

Snow covers theses ski jumps at Utah Olympic Park where the Ski Jumping, Nordic Combined, Skeleton, Luge and Bobsleigh events will take place in 2002. Brian Bahr/Allsport

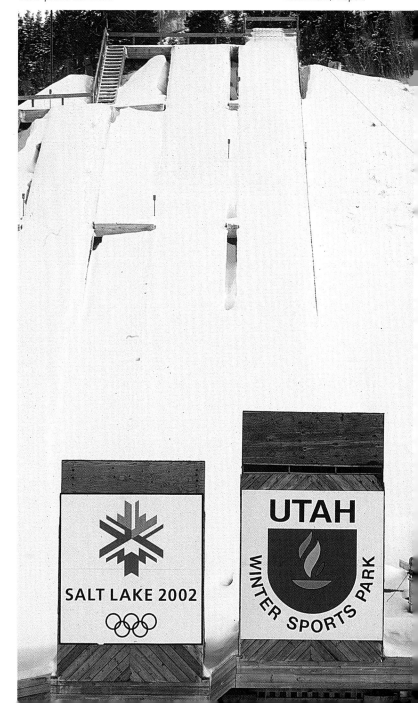

# DEER VALLEY

## LOCATION

Deer Valley is in Park City, which is approximately 48 kilometers (30 miles) from downtown Salt Lake City.

Deer Valley Resort is located in the quaint mountain town of Park City, UT.

© 2001 SLOC photo by David Quinney

## EVENTS

### SLALOM

### FREESTYLE AERIALS

### FREESTYLE MOGULS

The resort is spread over four mountains: Empire Canyon, Flagstaff, Bald, and Bald Eagle Mountains. The venue holds 20,000 spectators. The base altitude is 2,002 meters (6,570 feet) with a summit of 2,917 meters (9,570 feet) and a vertical drop of 914 meters (3,000 feet). The average annual snowfall is 762 centimeters (300 inches).

The U.S. Aerial Coach Matt Christensen has a lot of faith in his team and in Joe Pack, who won bronze at the '99 and '01 World Aerials Championship and is the '01 U.S. Aerials Champion.

"He's really stepped up to the plate," Christensen said about Pack. "He's got one thing on his mind [Olympic gold] and he's willing to sacrifice, to do what it takes to achieve it."

# E CENTER

## LOCATION

The E Center is located at 3200 South Decker Lake Drive in West Valley City.

said Doug Weight, a forward for Team USA and member of the St. Louis Blues. "That was a special thing. And we're looking for some redemption as a team and as a country."

The arena is a 28,000-square-meter (300,000-square-foot) indoor facility and is also the home to the Utah Grizzlies hockey team. The E Center holds 10,451 spectators.

Many U.S. spectators will be hoping for a three-time home-ice winning streak in 2002.

"To be in Salt Lake obviously will make you think back to Lake Placid [1980, when the U.S. men won gold],"

© 2001 SLOC photo by David Quinney

Both men's and women's Ice Hockey gold medal games will be played at the E Center.

© 2001 SLOC photo by David Quinney

# ICE SHEET AT OGDEN

## LOCATION

The Ice Sheet is located at 4390 Harrison Boulevard in Ogden. It is approximately 59 kilometers (36.6 miles) from the Olympic Village in Salt Lake City.

The Curling 2002 U.S. Olympic Trials will be held at the Ice Sheet in December 2001.

© 2001 SLOC photo by David Quinney

© 2001 SLOC photo by David Quinney

## EVENTS

**MEN'S AND WOMEN'S CURLING**

The Ice Sheet has four sheets of ice, each measuring 4.75 meters x 44.50 meters, and holds 2,000 spectators.

"The Ice Sheet is an excellent venue for Curling, once the Curling ice makers have worked their magic on the skating ice," David Garber, Executive Director of USA Curling, said. "While the venue has somewhat limited spectator capacity, this may bring the advantage, for those in the stands, of an intimate setting."

# PARK CITY MOUNTAIN RESORT

## LOCATION

The resort is located at 1310 Lowell Avenue in Park City, which is approximately 48 kilometers (30 miles) from downtown Salt Lake City.

Team USA's Picabo Street is Park City Mountain Resort's director of skiing.

© 2001 SLOC photo by David Quinney

The base of the resort is 2,117 meters (6,946 feet) and the summit is 2,530 meters (8,300.5 feet). The Halfpipe seating area holds 10,000 spectators and the Giant Slalom seating area holds 17,000 spectators. Picabo Street, winner of two Olympic medals, is the resort's director of skiing.

Freestyle snowboarder Tricia Byrnes is psyched about the 2002 Winter Games and the possibility of being there herself.

"I totally want to go to the Olympics," Byrnes said. "It would be awesome. That's the one time everyone tunes into winter sports. That's why I'm on the U.S. Team, that's why I'm working like this."

## EVENTS

**GIANT SLALOM**

**SNOWBOARDING PARALLEL**

**SNOWBOARDING HALFPIPE**

# PEAKS ICE ARENA

## LOCATION

The arena is located at 100 North Seven Peaks Boulevard in Provo. The venue is approximately 82 kilometers (51 miles) from the Olympic Village in Salt Lake City.

Set up against the foothills of the Wasatch Range, the Peaks Ice Arena will host the preliminary rounds of the men's and women's hockey tournaments. This ice arena measures 1,388 meters (4,550 feet) and is expected to hold 8,300 spectators.

Herb Brooks, veteran coach of the "Miracle on Ice" 1980 gold medal U.S. Olympic team, will return to coach the U.S. team in 2002. After being named head coach, Brooks seemed excited to be on the team.

"I'm extremely interested in the American hockey movement, and if USA Hockey feels I can help in this capacity at this time, I'm very proud to do so," Brooks said. "The Olympics are special and transcend other sporting events, although the competition will be extremely difficult. I believe in the American players. They'll play hard and smart, and they'll make a very good showing – one that we can all be proud of."

The Olympic Ice Hockey events will be played at the Peaks Ice Arena and at the E Center.
© 2001 SLOC photo by David Quinney

© 2001 SLOC photo by David Quinney

## EVENTS

### MEN'S AND WOMEN'S ICE HOCKEY

# RICE-ECCLES OLYMPIC STADIUM

## LOCATION

The stadium is located on the University of Utah campus at the corner of 400 South and 1400 East. It is a few blocks from the Olympic Village and public transportation from downtown will be provided.

Rice-Eccles Stadium is situated right up against the foothills of the Wasatch Range of the Rocky Mountains.
© 2001 SLOC photo by David Quinney

© 2001 SLOC photo by David Quinney

Rice-Eccles Stadium will be home to the Olympic Cauldron at the Opening Ceremonies on February 8, 2002. The stadium seating area has been expanded to hold 52,000 lucky spectators at the Opening and Closing Ceremonies. The projected worldwide television audience for the Opening and Closing Ceremonies is 3.5 billion.

The Closing Ceremony on February 24 will be built around the Salt Lake Organizing Committee's theme: "Light the Fire Within." The Closing Ceremony is expected to end with the customary fireworks celebration and passing of the torch to Greece, where the next Olympic Games will be celebrated in Athens in 2004. Home of the ancient Olympics, Athens has not seen an Olympic Games since the first Summer Olympic Games in 1896.

## EVENTS

### OPENING AND CLOSING CEREMONIES

# SALT LAKE ICE CENTER

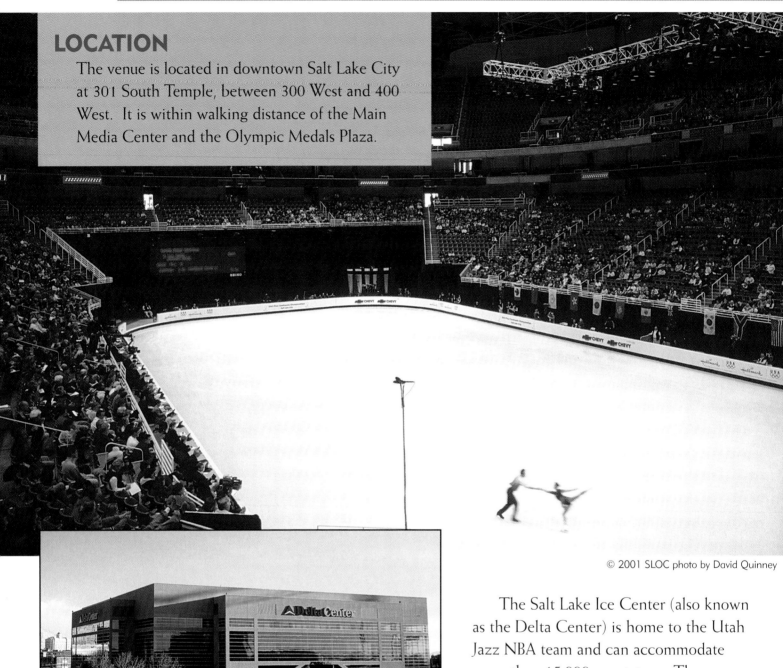

## LOCATION

The venue is located in downtown Salt Lake City at 301 South Temple, between 300 West and 400 West. It is within walking distance of the Main Media Center and the Olympic Medals Plaza.

© 2001 SLOC photo by David Quinney

The Salt Lake Ice Center is three blocks from Historic Temple Square where the Mormon Tabernacle Choir performs.

© 2001 SLOC photo by David Quinney

## EVENTS

**Figure Skating**

**Short-Track Speed Skating**

The Salt Lake Ice Center (also known as the Delta Center) is home to the Utah Jazz NBA team and can accommodate more than 15,000 spectators. The venue is six-stories high and is 4-hectare (10-acres) long. The high altitude and reduced air friction should make the Short-Track Speed Skating events very exciting. Look for record-breaking Speed Skating times at the Salt Lake Ice Center in 2002.

The U.S. Short-Track Speed Skating team is currently training at the U.S. Olympic Training Center in Colorado Springs, CO. where elevation is an important factor in training.

"The elevation in Colorado Springs is 6200'," Susan Ellis, the U.S. Short-Track coach, said. "Salt Lake City is 4200', so the athletes who train in Colorado Springs will be at an advantage having trained higher and then going lower. We have had camps in Salt Lake City and the athletes feel comfortable at that elevation."

# SNOWBASIN SKI RESORT

## LOCATION

Snowbasin is located east of Ogden in the Wasatch-Cache National Forest. The ski area is approximately 87 kilometers (54 miles) from the Olympic Village in downtown Salt Lake City.

Bernard Russi, the designer of the Downhill course, won gold in the Downhill event at the 1972 Olympic Winter Games in Sapporo, Japan.

© 2001 SLOC photo by David Quinney

Snowbasin boasts a Downhill course that is considered to be one of the top courses in the world. Designed by Swiss Olympic Downhill Champion Bernard Russi, the Downhill course has a 2,838-meter (9,311-foot) summit and an 881-meter vertical drop. The Downhill seating area will hold 23,500 spectators.

Super-G skiers will fly down nearly 2,000 vertical feet while turning through 30 to 35 gates, trying to beat the clock in less than 120 seconds. The seating area for both the Combined and Super-G events will hold 20,000 spectators.

"I want to be known as a guy who can win the big one," 2001 Super-G World Champion Daron Rahlves said. "It's like a dream. And it gives me the confidence to know I can do it at Snowbasin, too."

## EVENTS

### Downhill

### Combined Downhill/Slalom

### Super-G

# SOLDIER HOLLOW

## LOCATION

Soldier Hollow is 69 kilometers (43 miles) southeast of Salt Lake City and 10 kilometers (6 miles) west of Heber City.

The Biathlon 2002 U.S. Olympic Trials will be held at Soldier Hollow from December 26, 2001 to January 8, 2002.     © 2001 SLOC photo by David Quinney

## EVENTS

**BIATHLON**

**CROSS-COUNTRY SKIING**

**NORDIC COMBINED**

The Hollow is a 518-hectare (1,280-acre) mostly treeless site lying on the eastern edge of the Wasatch Mountain State Park. At 1,700 meters, Soldier Hollow is the highest elevation, world-class Biathlon venue in the world. The courses are a series of loops, and skiers will compete on different loops – or the same loop over and over again – depending on the event. About 90 percent of the courses are visible from the stadiums, which is much different than most venues where the skiers leave the stadium and are not seen again until they reenter the shooting range.

Rachel Steer, an Olympic hopeful from the U.S. Biathlon team, has had the advantage of practicing and competing at Soldier Hollow.

"I find a lot of my focus when I am out there shooting," Steer said. "I am putting so much emphasis on the wind there because I have found that it is very tricky, and that will be a weakness for people who haven't trained there. I focus a lot on what the flags are doing."

# UTAH OLYMPIC OVAL

This newly completed facility is the world's highest-altitude indoor skating oval. It has a unique cable-suspended system that eliminates the need for interior roof support. Long-Track Speed Skating requires a larger rink than Short-Track, so the Oval has an enclosed 400-meter track. The Oval is only one of six enclosed ovals in the world and will hold 6,500 spectators at the Winter Olympic Games.

Having hosted the World Single Distance Speed Skating Championships in March 2001, Utah Olympic Oval has already seen five of nine world records broken. The 2002 Olympic Winter

## LOCATION

The Oval is off of 4800 West in Kearns, which is about 45 minutes south of downtown Salt Lake City.

Games could solidify the Oval's reputation as having the fastest ice in the world.

"The U.S. Team is looking forward to competing at the Utah Olympic Oval," Bart Schouten, U.S. National Allround Coach, said. "It will be the fastest Oval in the world and the skaters love the speed. We are looking forward to setting World and American Records with the support of the home crowd.

It will be awesome to have the whole stadium filled with Americans and American flags. It will psych up the team and help us tremendously to perform better."

The Utah Olympic Oval will host the Long-Track Speed Skating 2002 U.S. Olympic Trials December 19-23, 2001.
© 2001 SLOC photo by David Quinney

© 2001 SLOC photo by David Quinney

## EVENTS

### LONG-TRACK
### SPEED SKATING

# UTAH OLYMPIC PARK

Utah Olympic Park holds the 15-turn Bobsleigh/Luge/Skeleton track and five regulation ski jumps. Several training jumps are used in the summer for demonstration and practice. A special pool just under the jumps is used as the landing pad. This park will accommodate 21,000 spectators for ski jumping events and 15,600 for track events.

The jumping hill at Utah Olympic Park is the highest World Cup Ski Jumping venue in the world at 7,350 feet. The Bobsleigh/Luge/Skeleton track is one of only three runs in North America and is used year-round for training purposes. The track is also being considered for the title of the world's fastest Luge track.

"The track in Park City is one of the fastest in the world," 2001 Luge World Championship bronze-medallist Tony Benshoof said. "From the men's start, sliders reach speeds in excess of 90 miles per hour, making it one of the most exciting tracks in the world to slide on. It takes both finesse and hard driving to make it down the track successfully and quick. Spectators can expect record speeds during the Olympic Games."

## LOCATION

Utah Olympic Park is approximately 53 kilometers (24 miles) east of downtown Salt Lake City off Interstate 80 east. The ski jumps are visible from the road.

© 2001 SLOC photo by John Wang

The Bobsleigh and Skeleton 2002 U.S. Olympic Trials will be held at Utah Olympic Park in December 2001 and January 2002.
© 2001 SLOC photo by David Quinney

## EVENTS

**BOBSLEIGH**

**LUGE**

**SKELETON**

**SKI JUMPING**

**NORDIC COMBINED**

**SALT LAKE 2002 VENUES AND TRANSPORTATION** Salt Lake City, Utah and surrounding areas

©2001 SLOC

**SALT LAKE 2002 OLYMPIC WINTER GAMES VENUES**

**1 The Ice Sheet at Ogden**
Curling

**2 Snowbasin Ski Area**
Downhill
Combined (Downhill/Slalom)
Super-G

**3 Salt Lake Ice Center**
Figure Skating
Short Track Speed Skating

**Olympic Medals Plaza**

**Main Media Center**

**4 E Center**
Ice Hockey

**5 Utah Olympic Oval**
Speed Skating

**6 Utah Olympic Park**
Bobsleigh
Luge
Skeleton
Ski Jumping
Nordic Combined (Ski Jumping)

**7 Park City Mountain Resort**
Giant Slalom
Snowboarding Halfpipe
Snowboarding
Parallel Giant Slalom

**8 Deer Valley Resort**
Slalom
Freestyle Aerials
Freestyle Moguls

**9 Soldier Hollow**
Biathlon
Cross-Country Skiing
Nordic Combined (Cross-Country Skiing)

**10 The Peaks Ice Arena**
Ice Hockey

**11 Rice-Eccles Olympic Stadium**

**Olympic Village**

**12 Salt Lake City International Airport**

**2002 CULTURAL OLYMPIAD VENUES**

**A Browning Center for the Performing Arts**
Weber State University,
3750 Harrison Boulevard, Ogden

**Peery's Egyptian Theater**
2415 Washington Boulevard, Ogden

**B Legacy Center**
Davis County Fair Park,
151 South 1100 West, Farmington

**C The George S. and Dolores Doré Eccles Center for the Performing Arts**
1750 Kearns Boulevard, Park City

**D Springville Museum of Art**
126 East 400 South, Springville

**E Abravanel Hall**
123 West South Temple, Salt Lake City

**Art Access Gallery**
339 West Pierpont Avenue, Salt Lake City

**Capitol Theatre**
50 West 200 South, Salt Lake City

**Salt Lake Art Center**
20 South West Temple, Salt Lake City

**Salt Lake City and County Building**
451 South State Street, Salt Lake City

**The Rio Grande**
300 South Rio Grande, Salt Lake City

**The Rose Wagner Performing Arts Center**
138 West Broadway, Salt Lake City

**The Salt Lake Tabernacle**
50 West South Temple, Salt Lake City

**F Kingsbury Hall**
University of Utah,
1395 East President's Circle, Salt Lake City

**Utah Museum of Natural History**
University of Utah,
1390 East President's Circle, Salt Lake City

**Utah Museum of Fine Arts**
University of Utah,
370 South 1530 East, Salt Lake City

**P Park and Ride/Walk Lots for Downtown Venues**

**P Park and Ride/Walk Lots for Outlying Venues**

ADA accessible parking and shuttle service will be available at all Park and Ride/Walk lots.

**VENUE DISTANCE AND TRAVEL TIMES**

| | Salt Lake Ice Center/MMC Olympic Medals Plaza | Rice-Eccles Olympic Stadium | Salt Lake City International Airport | Snowbasin Ski Area | The Ice Sheet at Ogden | The Peaks Ice Arena | E Center | Utah Olympic Oval | Utah Olympic Park | Park City Mountain Resort | Deer Valley Resort |
|---|---|---|---|---|---|---|---|---|---|---|---|
| Rice-Eccles Olympic Stadium | 5 km/3 mi 30 min | | | | | | | | | | |
| Salt Lake City International Airport | 11 km/7 mi 45 min | 17 km/10 mi 1 hr | | | | | | | | | |
| Snowbasin Ski Area | 70 km/44 mi 2 hr | 75 km/47 mi 2 hr | 77 km/48 mi 2 hr | | | | | | | | |
| The Ice Sheet at Ogden | 59 km/37 mi 1 hr 30 min | 66 km/41 mi 1 hr 45 min | 53 km/33 mi 1 hr 15 min | 34 km/20 mi 1 hr 15 min | | | | | | | |
| The Peaks Ice Arena | 78 km/49 mi 1 hr 30 min | 74 km/46 mi 1 hr 45 min | 77 km/48 mi 1 hr 30 min | 136 km/85 mi 2 hr 45 min | 128 km/79 mi 2 hr 15 min | | | | | | |
| E Center | 14 km/9 mi 45 min | 20 km/12 mi 1 hr | 14 km/9 mi 45 min | 82 km/50 mi 2 hr | 73 km/45 mi 1 hr 30 min | 67 km/41 mi 1 hr 45 min | | | | | |
| Utah Olympic Oval | 22 km/14 mi 1 hr | 27 km/17 mi 1 hr | 17 km/10 mi 45 min | 90 km/56 mi 2 hr 15 min | 82 km/51 mi 1 hr 45 min | 65 km/40 mi 1 hr 30 min | 11 km/7 mi 45 min | | | | |
| Utah Olympic Park | 45 km/28 mi 2 hr 15 min | 38 km/24 mi 2 hr | 53 km/33 mi 2 hr | 100 km/62 mi 2 hr 30 min | 104 km/65 mi 2 hr 30 min | 83 km/52 mi 2 hr 30 min | 47 km/29 mi 2 hr | 56 km/35 mi 2 hr 15 min | | | |
| Park City Mountain Resort | 54 km/34 mi 2 hr | 48 km/30 mi 2 hr | 64 km/39 mi 2 hr 15 min | 109 km/68 mi 2 hr | 114 km/71 mi 2 hr 30 min | 83 km/48 mi 2 hr 15 min | 77 km/48 mi 2 hr 15 min | 58 km/35 mi 2 hr 15 min | 5 km/3 mi 1 hr 15 min | | |
| Deer Valley Resort | 58 km/36 mi 2 hr 15 min | 52 km/32 mi 2 hr | 66 km/41 mi 2 hr 15 min | 113 km/70 mi 2 hr 30 min | 117 km/73 mi 2 hr 30 min | 80 km/50 mi 2 hr | 59 km/37 mi 2 hr 15 min | 68 km/42 mi 2 hr | 17 km/10 mi 45 min | 6 km/4 mi 45 min | |
| Soldier Hollow | 86 km/53 mi 2 hr 30 min | 74 km/46 mi 2 hr 30 min | 94 km/58 mi 2 hr 30 min | 129 km/80 mi 2 hr 15 min | 145 km/90 mi 3 hr | 46 km/29 mi 1 hr 45 min | 88 km/54 mi 2 hr 30 min | 96 km/60 mi 2 hr 15 min | 48 km/30 mi 1 hr 30 min | 45 km/28 mi 1 hr 15 min | 45 km/28 mi 1 hr 45 min |

Travel times shown are realistic estimates of how long it will take you to travel between venues, park your car, walk to a venue gate or walk to the shuttle bus boarding area and ride the shuttle to a venue gate. Please plan accordingly.

© 2001 SLOC

A general view of Park City, UT which is nestled in the Wasatch Mountains.
Mike Powell/Allsport

# Sport-By-Sport Preview

Picabo Street seems to truly be flying at the March 2001 Alpine Championships in Whitefish, Montana.

Adam Pretty/AUS/Allsport

## ALPINE SKIING

Austrian Hermann Maier clowns around with Erik Schlopy at the 2001 Skiing World Cup event in Sweden.     Zoom/Allsport

Alpine Skiing gets its name from the Alps, where downhill skiing spread in the mid 1800s after developing as a sport in Norway.

The object of Alpine Skiing is simple: start at the gate and get to the bottom as fast as possible.  The differences between the various events are based on the differing courses.

There are ten Alpine events (five for men and five for women): the Downhill, Super Giant Slalom (Super-G), Giant Slalom, Slalom, and Combined.

The Downhill event has the longest course, reaching the highest speeds.  Skiers have one run down one course containing a few gates placed on the course to help maintain speed and direction.

The Super-G event has the speed of the Downhill combined with the tight, precise turns found in Giant Slalom. Skiers have one run down a 700-meter course that has 30 gates.

The Giant Slalom is a looser version of the Slalom with wider, fewer turns. Skiers have two runs down two different courses.

The Slalom is held on the shortest course with the quickest turns. Skiers have two runs down two courses. The first course has hinged break-away poles that the skiers must zig-zag around with great precision. The second course is designed for speed: it's an all-out sprint to the finish. Winners are determined by the best total time from both courses.

The Combined event puts one Downhill and two Slalom runs together. The winner is determined by the total times from all three runs.

Picabo Street will once again be one to watch in her third Olympic appearance. Street won Olympic silver in 1994 in the Downhill with a time of 1:36.59, just behind German Katja Seizinger who had a time of 1:35.93. Street also won gold in the Super-G with a time of 1:18.02 in the same year.

Street will be expecting her greatest competitors from Switzerland and Croatia in 2002. Sonja Nef is aiming for gold in 2002 after winning the World Cup Giant Slalom title. Janica Kostelic will be another woman to watch in 2002. This 19-year-old from Croatia became the second-youngest World Cup title-holder in history after winning the overall title in 2001.

Team USA's Erik Schlopy leans into the gate to come in second during the men's Giant Slalom 2000-2001 World Cup race in Italy.
Allsport UK/Allsport

On the men's side, Daron Rahlves stands a good chance of reaching the medal stand since his January 2001 Super-G gold-medal victory at the World Alpine Championships in St. Anton, Austria. Rahlves' biggest competitor is Austrian Hermann Maier who shattered his right leg in a motorcycle accident in August of 2001. Maier should not be counted out, though. He returned from an amazing crash at the Nagano Winter Games to win gold in the Super-G and Giant Slalom. He also swept the 2000-2001 World Cup with overall, Downhill, Super-G and Giant Slalom titles.

Other U.S. athletes to watch at the 2002 Games are Erik Schlopy and Kristina Koznick. Schlopy placed 15th in World Cup overall standings and Koznick placed seventh in Slalom and 17th overall.

Team USA members hope to stay healthy and stand as a united front on their home snow in 2002.

# BIATHLON

Techniques to lower the heart rate help biathletes shoot straight after skiing as hard as they can.
Zoom/Allsport

Antje Harvey of Germany shoots with precision in the women's 4x7.5 Biathlon event at the 1994 Olympic Winter Games in Lillehammer, Norway.
Pascal Rondeau /Allsport

Skis used as a means of transportation have been around for millennia. Wooden ski fragments found in Sweden have been dated to 4,000 years ago. The sport of Biathlon has traditionally been used for means outside of recreation, as shown in ancient Nordic rock carvings depicting men on skis hunting animals.

An important part of military life from the 1700s on, Biathlon has been taught since then as a form of national protection in northern European countries. In fact, the sport was introduced as a military exercise at the very first Olympic Winter Games in 1924.

There are eight events in Biathlon (four for men and four for women). The men's events are the 10 km Sprint, 12.5 km Pursuit, 20 km Individual, and the 4 x 7.5 km Relay. The women's events are the 7.5 km Sprint, 10 km Pursuit, 15 km Individual, and the 4 x 7.5 km Relay.

In the Sprint, biathletes ski and stop twice at the firing ranges to shoot at targets 50 meters away. They must hit all five targets with five bullets or take one lap around the 150-meter penalty loop for each target missed.

In the Pursuit, the athletes stop four times and must hit five targets with five bullets. Any missed shots are penalized with a lap around the 150-meter penalty loop. The athletes in the Pursuit all start within five minutes, and the lead may change five or six times during the race since the loops are very short and shooting must be done quickly and accurately.

The Pursuit is making its Olympic debut at the 2002 Salt Lake Winter Games and is sure to be an exciting addition. In fact, the inclusion of the Pursuit has given more European television coverage to the sport, making it the number one watched and rated sport on Eurosport in the winter months.

The Individual is like the Pursuit in that the skiers stop four times and must hit five targets with five bullets, but the penalty for missing is different. For every missed target, one minute is added to the athlete's total time.

The Relay consists of a four-person team each skiing 7.5 km legs. Each person has two firing sequences and is given three extra bullets, which must be loaded one at a time to hit five targets. The penalty for each target missed is a lap around the 150-meter penalty loop.

The courses vary for men and women. Female biathletes usually shoot at their first target after skiing two or 2.5 kilometers with additional targets between two and three kilometers apart. The men will first shoot after skiing 2.5 to four kilometers with additional targets between 2.5 and 3.5 kilometers apart.

The prone shooting position is used in the first and third station in the Individual events, as well as the first station in the Sprint events. The standing shooting position is used otherwise. A .22-caliber rifle has been used as the official rifle caliber since 1978.

The Russian and Nordic nations have dominated the sport since its Olympic inception in 1980. The German, French, and Ukrainian teams are also worthy adversaries. The top rated woman in the world for the past four years is Magdalena Forsberg of Sweden and the top man is Raphael Poiree of France.

The top U.S. prospect for 2002 is Jeremy Teela who placed ninth in the Sprint in the 2001 World Championships. Jay Hakkinen, who placed seventh in December 2000 in Oberhof, Germany, and Rachel Steer, who placed 23rd and 27th at the World Championships, will also do their best to make a big impression in Biathlon.

"I'm looking at 2002 and I'm putting all my eggs in one basket," Teela said. "I'm giving Biathlon everything I've got."

Team USA's Joan Smith skis with her gun strapped to her back in the 15K event at the '94 Lillehammer Olympic Winter Games.
Nathan Bilow/Allsport

# BOBSLEIGH

Evidence unearthed prior to the Nagano Games in 1998 shows lumber sleds used in Albany, N.Y. in the 1880s, but the Swiss contend that bobsleighs originated in their country around the same time. Whatever the case may be, bobsleighs have been used for work and play for hundreds of years.

The sport was featured at the first 1924 Olympic Winter Games in Chamonix, France just one year after the sport's governing body was founded. It has been included in the Winter Games ever since, with one exception. The sport was not included in the 1960 Games in Squaw Valley because no track was built.

Bobsleigh has seen many variations over the years – from 2-man to 5-man, and prone to sitting position – and will see another change in 2002 when the 2-woman event is added to the lineup. Even the name of the sport is different: in Europe, it's called Bobsleigh, and in the U.S. it's Bobsled. Both uses will probably be used at the 2002 Winter Games.

For the Salt Lake Games, there will be three events: the 2-man, 4-man, and the inaugural 2-woman. The 2-man and 4-man events will consist of four runs timed to hundredths of a second. Each

Driver Jean Racine high fives coach Tuffield Latour as they finished third in the February 2001 Women's Bobsleigh World Cup at Utah Olympic Park in Park City, UT.    Doug Pensinger/Allsport

Brian Shimer and Randy Jones in USA
2 shoot down the track in Lillehammer.

team will have two runs per day. The 2-woman event will be held on one day, and each team will have two runs timed to hundredths of a second.

Each country may enter a maximum of two sleds per event. Although the teams have not been chosen, Todd Hays' 2-man and 4-man teams stand a good chance of being U.S. entries. Hays won gold in the 4-man and bronze in the 2-man at Lake Placid, NY in March 2001. The German and Swiss teams in both 2- and 4-man will give the U.S. the strongest competition in 2002. German Andre Lange finished the 2001 season first and Swiss Martin Annen finished second overall in World Cup points.

Jen Davidson and Jean Racine, who have raced on the track at Utah Olympic Park and won, are favored to win gold in 2002. Racine and Davidson

Pascal Rondeau/Allsport

won six of seven 2000-2001 World Cup events and won the overall title for the second year in a row. The second sled in the 2-woman event will be between Bonnie Warner and Vonetta Flowers, and Jill Bakken and Kristi McGihon. These two 2-woman teams placed second and third respectively, behind Davidson and Racine at the World Cup finale in Utah. Look for Team USA's women to dominate the medals stand in Salt Lake.

Track stars sometimes become brakemen because they are able to give the best initial push-off.       Vandystadt/Allsport

# CROSS-COUNTRY SKIING

These two Cross-Country skiers are using the freestyle technique, pushing off to the sides to propel them forward.

Allsport

The original Nordic ski sport, Cross-Country has been a part of history for over 5,000 years. Skis were originally used as a transportation device and a means to hunt for food throughout Europe and Asia. In fact, skiing as a sport and not a necessity did not come about until the 19th century in Norway.

Cross-Country skiing has traditionally had the one classic technique of a straight stride within two parallel tracks. But in 1982, Vermonter Bill Koch made freestyle skiing, which is much faster than the classical style, a popular technique. Today's freestyle technique uses both legs to push off and seemingly "skate" across the snow at a rapid pace.

Skiing styles and distances differentiate the 12 Cross-Country events. The men's events are the 1.5 km Sprint, 15 km Classic, 30 km Freestyle, 50 km Classic, Combined Pursuit, and 4 x 10 km

Relay. The women's events are the 1.5 km Sprint, 10 km Classic, 15 km Freestyle, 30 km Classic, Combined Pursuit, and 4 x 5 km Relay. During the Relay, the skiers must use the classic style in the first two legs, and freestyle in the last two legs.

Several new and old events have been added to the list of Cross-Country events for 2002. Both the men's and women's 1.5 km Sprint will be contested for the first time in 2002, and the men's 15 km Classic and women's 10 km Classic return to the Winter Games after a 14-year absence.

Team USA is looking to have at least a few top-ten finishes, but three athletes are aiming for the podium in 2002. Two-time Olympians Justin Wadsworth and Marcus Nash were college teammates for a year in the '90s in Utah and have been U.S. teammates since the '94 Winter Games.

Nina Kemppel, who is looking forward to being the first female Cross-Country athlete to compete in four Olympic Games, enjoys the health benefits of the sport and wants to make 2002 her best year so far.

"Cross-Country gets you in the best shape of any sport," Kemppel said. "Your cardiovascular conditioning is so high, and although you may not be as fast as someone else – I'll get those Russian girls one day – Cross-Country's so good for your body."

Bjoern Daehlie of Norway and Niklas Jonsson of Sweden compete in the men's 50 K Free Cross-Country event at the '98 Nagano Games in which they won gold and silver.                    Jed Jacobsohn/Allsport

# CURLING

Although Curling only made its official Olympic debut at the 1998 Nagano Winter Games, the sport dates back to 16th century Scotland. Originally, curling stones were called "Kuting Stones" and were found already worn smooth by moving water. The player would push the stone with a twist to make it "curl" across the ice. Brooms were used to clear snow, and are now used with vigor to polish the ice, making the stone curl less and travel farther. The sport was brought to North America in the mid-1700s by British troops and has become very popular in the northern U.S. and Canada.

At the Olympic Games, ten qualifying countries in men's and women's team competition will compete in a round- robin tournament. The results of the round-robin will determine advancement to the semifinals. The winners of the semifinals will play the gold-medal game, and the losers of the semifinals will play the bronze-medal game.

Each team has four members: the lead, second, vice-skip, and skip. The skip is the captain of the team and usually shoots last. The skip also directs the other teammates on strategy.

Curling has elements of finesse that evoke another Scottish game - golf. It has also been referred to as "chess on ice" because of the great deal of strategy involved.

Two members of the Swedish team use their brooms to manipulate the direction and speed of the stone towards the house.

Mike Hewitt/Allsport

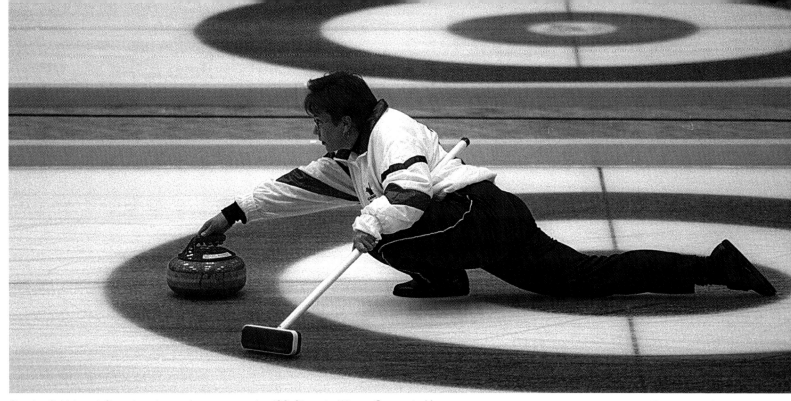

Sandra Schirler of Canada releases her stone at the '98 Olympic Winter Games in Nagano.

Gary M. Prior/Allsport

Two teams of four members play against each other. Each player, alternately, delivers a 42-pound stone down the ice toward a series of concentric circles known as the "house."

Each member gets very low to the ice and uses the handle to gently impart a twist on the stone as it slides down the ice, while the two other teammates sweep if needed for distance and direction. Each member delivers two stones, so a total of 16 stones go down the ice in one end, or inning. The two teams compete to get their stones closest to the center circle of the house, called the "tee." A point is given for each stone closer to the tee than the opponent's stones. Players are allowed to bump their opponent's stones out of the way or even off the playing field. The score is tallied after each end, and 10 ends make up one complete game.

Canada was a formidable foe in Nagano, coming up gold in the women's tournament and silver in the men's. Their men's and women's teams were also World Champions in 2001. The Swiss and Swedish teams also look to win big in Curling. The Swiss men's team won gold in Nagano, beating the Canadian team 9-3.

The U.S. Olympic Team Trials will take place in Ogden, UT at the future Olympic venue, The Ice Sheet, Dec. 11-16, 2001. Team USA, which finished 4th (men's) and 5th (women's) at Nagano, hopes to better its standing in 2002. Team USA currently ranks 4th (women's) and 5th (men's) in the world, based on Olympic ranking points in the last three World Championships.

With three silver and two bronze medals in the last 10 years of World Championships, Team USA is considered to be a medal contender in both men's and women's Curling competition in Salt Lake City.

Allsport Hulton Deutsch/Allsport

This 1943 Curling match on the rink attached to the Wimbledon Royal Golf Club shows that even regular brooms can be used in a game.

# FIGURE SKATING

Michelle Kwan demonstrates her graceful abilities that she will use at the XIXth Olympic Winter Games in Salt Lake City.
Doug Pensinger/Allsport

Figure Skating has always been a crowd-pleaser since its inception and debut in the 1908 Summer Olympic Games in London. America has seen its share of winning figure skaters – from Dick Button's amazing double axel jump to win gold in 1948 at St. Moritz, to Kristi Yamaguchi's triumph over four top-ranked rivals to win gold at Albertville in 1992. In fact, the U.S. has the most Olympic Figure Skating medals with 40 total.

There are four events in Figure Skating: men's and ladies Singles, Pairs, and Ice Dancing.

The Singles event is a showcase for technical skill and graceful form. Athletes compete in the short program, worth 33.3 percent of the final score, and the free skate, worth 66.7 percent of the final score.

The Pairs event also has a short program and free-skate with the same score percentage. The short program in both Singles and Pairs competition must not exceed two minutes and 40 seconds. Pairs skaters must also perform their routine in unison while executing complex lifts, spins, and throw jumps while keeping exact time.

Ice Dancing is divided into three segments: two compulsory dances, a two-minute original dance, and a four-minute free dance. Each team performs the same two pre-determined compulsory dances, each worth 10 percent of the team's final score. Judges watch everything from placement of dance steps, to unison and expression.

In the original dance, teams are given a specific rhythm and tempo range chosen annually by the International Skating Union (ISU) and must make up their own unique version of the dance. The original dance is worth 30 percent of the final score.

Skaters are given free range in the free dance segment. Each dance team chooses their own music and uses intricate dance holds, footwork, and changes of position to impress the judges. The free dance makes up 50 percent of the team's final score.

U.S. Pairs skaters to watch this winter are two-time U.S. champions Kyoko Ina and John Zimmerman. In the Ice Dancing events, look to three-time U.S. champions Naomi Lang and Peter Tchernyshev to give the Russians some competition.

U.S. women have dominated the Singles competition, winning one-third of the medals in this event in Winter Olympic history. Michelle Kwan and her teammates hope to add to this tally by dominating the medals stand in Salt Lake.

Kwan, who picked up her fourth World Championship title in 2001, hopes to best her

Todd Eldredge spins on the ice he will see again in February at the 2002 Olympic Winter Games.          Brian Bahr/Allsport

Nagano silver with a gold in 2002. Kwan will have some competition in three-time World silver medallist Irina Slutskaya of Russia who has claimed victory over Kwan at the past two ISU Grand Prix final events heading into the Olympic season.

Also hoping to contend for an Olympic medal is 2001 World bronze medallist Sarah Hughes, one of the most consistent performers on the world stage the past three seasons. A veteran of three World Championships, Angela Nikodinov rounds out this dynamic U.S. trio with her fifth place finish at the 2001 World Championships.

Team USA's men also stand a good chance for medals in the Singles competition. Two-time U.S. Olympian Todd Eldredge will again battle for the gold in Salt Lake, and will be joined by teammates Timothy Goebel who finished fourth just behind Eldredge at the 2001 World Championships, and two-time World bronze medallist Michael Weiss. The U.S. men's greatest foes are Russian duo Evgeni Plushenko and Alexei Yagudin who have combined to win the last four World titles and placed first and second respectively at the 2001 World Champs in Vancouver, B.C.

Nevertheless, the U.S. men and women have their sights set on gold in 2002. Look for the Figure Skating medal events to be some of the most popular events at the XIXth Olympic Winter Games.

Italians Barbara Fusar Poli and Maurizio Margaglio took home the gold in the free dance competition at the 2001 World Figure Skating Championships in Vancouver.          Brian Bahr/Allsport

# FREESTYLE SKIING

Born out of 1960s America, Freestyle Skiing combines technical Alpine skiing and daredevil acrobatics. The format originally consisted of squeezing ballet, moguls, and aerial maneuvers into one run, thus the "free" style of skiing.

Two events make up today's Olympic Freestyle Skiing: men's and women's Moguls and men's and women's Aerials.

In Moguls competition, the athletes ski down a field of snowy bumps (called moguls) including two mid-course jumps. Moguls skiers are judged on their turns, air (or jumps), and speed. Turns make up 50 percent of their score, air 25 percent, and speed 25 percent.

Jonny Moseley of the United States in action during the men's moguls at the Olympic Winter Games in Nagano, Japan. Moseley went on to win the gold medal in this event.

Team USA's Hannah Hardaway demonstrates her skill during the 2001 FIS Freestyle World Championships in Whistler, Canada.

Not only do Moguls skiers have to master the moguls and come up with creative jumps, they must complete the run with a good time and ski the moguls in the cleanest, most efficient manner.

"Moguls puts everything in one package," Jonny Moseley, '98 Olympic and World Cup champ, said. "Your run has the excitement of speeding down the hill, the freedom of aerials and the skill in the bumps – just a rush all the way."

Aerialists have a choice of jumps at different heights, based on what type of jump they will perform. They can be as high as four meters, with takeoff angles as steep as 70 degrees. Since the height of their jumps can be as high as a four-story building, the Aerialists' landing area is made

Nathan Bilow/Allsport

up of soft, churned snow to absorb the impact.

The scoring components of Aerials are 20 percent air, 50 percent form, and 30 percent landing. The total score is the sum of the three components multiplied by the jump's degree of difficulty.

Freestyle skiing made its debut at the '92 Albertville Olympic Games when Moguls was added to the lineup. Due to the success of Moguls and the urgings of Olympic and ski organizations, Aerials was added to the Olympic roster in 1994 at Lillehammer. Since 1992, a U.S. Olympian has medalled in at least one Freestyle event. At the Nagano Winter Games in 1998, U.S. skiers took

Team USA's Joe Pack always keeps his eye on the ground when performing his difficult mid-air maneuvers.

Matthew Stockman/Allsport

three of the four Olympic gold medals in Freestyle skiing – Moseley winning Moguls with Eric Bergoust and Nikki Stone taking the men's and women's Aerials titles.

Moseley will return to the world stage in February 2002 after taking two years off. After winning silver behind Moseley, Finland's Janne Lahtela has lead the World Cup standings for the past three seasons. The U.S. Moguls team still stands a good chance to medal with teammates Moseley and '00 U.S. moguls champion Evan Dybvig.

Gold medallist Bergoust has been busy adding the title of 2001 Aerial World Champion, second overall, to his growing list of accomplishments. Joe Pack has consistently nipped at Bergoust's heels this past season, placing second in the Aerial World Championships and third overall. It will be interesting to see these two friends battle it out for podium placement at Deer Valley Resort in 2002.

Donna Weinbrecht will be returning in 2002 after winning the first Olympic Moguls gold medal at the '92 Albertville Games. Weinbrecht will be cheering on U.S. teammates Ann Battelle, the '99 and '00 overall World Cup Moguls champion, and Hannah Hardaway, who finished third in the Moguls World Cup standings and seventh overall.

U.S. Aerialist Emily Cook, who placed sixth in Aerials World Cup standings, will be watching out for the Aerialist from down under, Australian Jacqui Cooper. Cooper, along with World Moguls Champion Kari Traa, will be the women's toughest competition in 2002.

# ICE HOCKEY

Team USA's men's and women's Hockey teams will have to battle against the world's best in 2002.                    Allsport

Brought to Canada by the British, Ice Hockey remains as one of the most popular winter sports in the world. The sport found its way to the U.S. in the 1890s and the first reported U.S. game was between Johns Hopkins and Yale Universities in 1895.

The U.S. has a rich Olympic Hockey history, winning amazing gold-medal games in 1960 and 1980. The 1960 U.S. Olympic team – comprised of carpenters, insurance agents, a fireman and an ad salesman – came out of nowhere to win gold in Squaw Valley, CA. The 1980 U.S. team broke the former Soviet Union's 16-year winning streak and brought pride back to the hearts of the home crowd with their victory.

Olympic Ice Hockey has two events, the men's and women's tournaments. Fourteen teams will battle through three rounds for the men's title and eight teams going through two rounds will determine the women's champion.

The 2002 men's teams already slated for the final round based on their finish at the '98 Nagano Games are: Czech Republic, Russia, Finland, Canada, Sweden, and the United States. Eight other teams will play in the preliminary round to determine which teams will get the two remaining positions in the final round. These eight teams are chosen to participate in the Olympic Winter Games based on their finishes at the '99 International Ice Hockey Federation (IIHF) World Championships and the Olympic qualification tournaments in February 2001.

The eight teams in the 2002 Olympic women's tournament are Canada, United States, Finland, Sweden, Russia, China, Kazakhstan, and Germany. The first six teams in the above list qualified for the 2002 Winter Games by finishing in the top final placings from the 2000 IIHF World Championships. Kazakhstan and Germany qualified at the Olympic qualifying tournament in February 2001.

At the Olympics, IIHF rules are followed. Some of them differ from NHL rules, and will be noticeable. For instance, the rink dimensions. The IIHF rink is 13.5 feet wider and the goal lines are

At the inaugural women's Olympic Hockey finals in 1998, the U.S. women took home the event's first gold medal. The U.S. and Canadian teams have historically been evenly matched. The Canadians have beaten the U.S. in seven consecutive World Championships, but Cammi Granato and her teammates plan to show the world they are worth another gold at Salt Lake City in 2002. The women's Hockey finals are projected to be an exciting match-up between these long-time rivals.

Herb Brooks, the coach of the legendary "Miracle on Ice" 1980 U.S. Olympic Team, has returned to coach the men's team. He hopes to lead the men's team to the podium stand in 2002 after they were eliminated in the qualification round at Nagano.

Another familiar face will be Detroit Red Wing Chris Chelios who will return to the role of Team USA captain. The Canadian and Russian teams are expected to be the toughest competitors, having a combined 14 out of 19 Olympic gold medals. Also look for the Swedish team to make a strong competitive effort as well.

Both the men and women's Ice Hockey finals are expected to be thrilling, especially if Team USA can win two gold medals on their home ice.

13 feet, as opposed to 11 feet, from each end of the rink. This allows for a more wide-open style of play, potentially higher scoring games, and more action behind the goal.

One other thing to watch for: there are no commercial breaks in Olympic Hockey, so the teams must play the full 20-minute period before getting a rest. Look for this element combined with a bigger rink to make a difference in the performance of some NHL hockey players who are returning to the Olympic Games for only the second time.

Jaromir Jagr and his Czechoslovakian teammates will be defending their Olympic title in Salt Lake City.

Brian Bahr/Allsport

# LUGE

Record times are expected in Luge since Utah Olympic Park boasts the fastest Luge track in the world.　© 2001 SLOC photo by David Quinney

Historical findings have unearthed the possibility of Viking sleds as early as 800 A.D. These sleds are even believed to have two runners, much like those used today.

The Olympic Luge competition is comprised of men's Singles, women's Singles, and Doubles medal events. Although the Doubles event is open to both sexes, Olympic participants have always been men.

The Singles events take place over two days, two runs per day. Doubles competitors have two runs on one day of competition. Time is measured to a single thousandth (.001) of a second, which makes Luge and Short-Track Speed Skating the most precisely timed sports in the Olympic Winter Games. The fastest total time for both Singles and Doubles determines the winner of the event.

Basically, a slider will go feet-first down the track

at Utah Olympic Park that is 1,316 meters-long featuring 17 curves. Luge athletes steer the sled by using both their legs and shoulders, depending on the turn. In Doubles, the person on top rests on a small seat and the chest of the person underneath. Since sight is limited for the bottom driver, slight head movements from the top driver signal upcoming turns.

The 2002 Luge events are sure to be thrilling, since the Utah Olympic Park, which opened in 1997, boasts the fastest Luge track in the world.

"Because this is a combined track (built for Luge, Bobsled and Skeleton) the distance between curves is greater," Chris Thorpe, '98 silver medallist in Doubles, said. "This allows for sliders to reach speeds in excess of 90 miles per hour. Those speeds keep the athletes on their toes."

The three Luge events have been a part of every Olympic Winter Games since 1964 with 88 out of 90 medals awarded to athletes from Italy, Austria, Germany, and the former Soviet Union. Who were the two exceptions? Team USA brought home the Doubles silver and bronze at Nagano in 1998.

Thorpe and new partner Clay Ives hope to better Thorpe's silver medal success he shared with former partner Gordy Sheer. Joining them are '98 Olympic bronze-medallists Mark Grimmette and Brian Martin, who finished fourth in last season's overall World Cup standings behind the Germans.

Italian Armin Zöggeler led the World Cup men's Singles category last season. One of Team USA's best, Tony Benshoof finished with a career-best eighth place overall.

The women are lead by the German sliders who

Team USA's Christopher Thorpe, seen here with Gorden Sheer, will compete with new teammate Clay Ives in 2002.                      Mike Powell/Allsport

finished first and second in last season's overall World Cup. Courtney Zablocki lead Team USA with an eighth place overall finish.

Look for exciting action as the world's best sliders take on the fastest Luge track in the world at the Olympic Winter Games.

This slider whisks around one of the final turns at Utah Olympic Park.                      Brian Bahr/Allsport

# NORDIC COMBINED

Hannu Manninen of Finland skis hard to maintain his lead in the men's Nordic Combined 15K Cross-Country race at Snow Harp during the 1998 Olympic Winter Games.                    Zoom/Allsport

The sport of Nordic Combined, like many other Alpine and Nordic events, has been a part of the Olympic Winter Games since the inaugural 1924 Games in Chamonix, France. Nordic Combined was popular at the ski carnivals in Norway, and as a result, the Norwegians have taken home both the most Olympic medals (24) and gold medals (11).

Three events make up Nordic Combined: the Individual, Sprint and Team events. In the Individual, skiers jump twice from a 90-meter hill on the first day, and compete in a 15-kilometer race on the second day of competition.

Sprinters first jump from the large hill, which measures 120 meters high. They then compete in the 7.5 km all-out sprint on the second day. The

Christian Hoffmann of Austria (left) finished first ahead of Johann Muehlegg of Spain (right) during the 30K U.S. Nordic Cup event at Soldier Hollow in January 2001.       Matthew Stockman/Allsport

Sprint event will be making its Olympic debut in 2002.

Team competition consists of all four skiers individually jumping twice off of the normal 90-meter hill. The second day of competition consists of a 4 x 5 km Relay Race. The winner in all three events is the first person to cross the finish line in the ski race. The freestyle type of skiing is allowed throughout all three events.

Also called "the decathlon of skiing," the Nordic Combined requires both strength for jumping and quickness for skiing.

"It's a real bear, but it's fun too," said Tom Tetreault, a three-time Olympian and three-time national champion who retired after the '99 season.

In a sport dominated by the Nordic countries, Todd Lodwick looks like Team USA's best chance for a medal. Lodwick finished the season in sixth place overall and has finished in the top eight in the last four years in World Cup competition.

Bill Demong, who produced his first World Cup top-10 finish in 2001, hopes to continue his success right into the Olympic Winter Games in 2002. This native New Yorker finished the '01 season with six top-15 finishes, won his first two U.S. titles, and finished 16th in World Cup points.

The leading men of Nordic Combined are

Todd Lodwick of the U.S. team seems to be flying out of the Olympic rings at the Nagano Olympic Winter Games. Al Bello/Allsport

Norwegian Bjarte Engen Vik and Austrian Felix Gottwald. Vik is the returning gold medallist in both the individual and team events. Gottwald won the overall 2001 World Cup title in March at Oslo, Norway. Both of these men stand a good chance of fighting it out for the gold in 2002, but shouldn't count out Team USA's Lodwick as a strong competitor.

This photo taken at the '89 Nordic World Ski Championships in Lahti, Finland shows just how high the jumpers can fly.

# SKELETON

A racer passes under the finish line at the 2001 Skeleton World Cup held at Utah Olympic Park.

Doug Pensinger/Allsport

Skeleton, which is considered the world's first sliding sport, is named after a new metal design that was introduced in 1892 that was so simple and bare, people said it looked like a skeleton.

Performed facedown in the prone position, Skeleton athletes have to work against G-forces to keep their chins off the ice. The athletes use slight neck and shoulder shifts to maneuver around curves in the track.

Skeleton's brief Olympic history has seen U.S. medallists both times it has been contested. American brothers Jennison and John Heaton won the gold and silver medals at the 1928 Winter Games in St. Moritz.

John came back to St. Moritz 20 years later in 1948 to repeat his silver medal success when he learned Skeleton was again included in the Winter Games.

In 2002, men's Skeleton will be contested for the first time as an Olympic event outside of St. Moritz, where the sport was founded in the 1800s. The women's event will be contested for the first time ever at the Salt Lake Winter Games.

Thanks in large part to the Heaton brothers, the United States has three out of six Olympic Skeleton medals. Team USA hopes to prove its continued dominance of the sport with their ace-in-the-hole, Lincoln DeWitt. DeWitt is currently ranked number one in the world,

February at Canada Olympic Park in Calgary.

Skeleton spectators at Utah Olympic Park in 2002 are in for a treat, witnessing the excitement of the Olympic sport for the first time outside of Switzerland.

Left: The Earl of Northesk (left) of Great Britain and Jennison Heaton of the USA prepare for the Skeleton Bobsleigh event at the 1928 Winter Olympic Games in St. Moritz, Switzerland. Heaton won the gold, his brother John won silver, and the Earl won bronze.

IOC Olympic Museum /Allsport

Below: Tricia Stumpf of Team USA hopes to be the first woman to win gold at the inaugural women's event.

Matthew Stockman/Allsport

having won his first World Cup in February 2001 on the future Olympic track in Park City.

Joining DeWitt on the team will be Jim Shea, Jr. who placed third in the world after the 2000-2001 season and if he qualifies, will be a third-generational Olympian. Shea's father competed at Innsbruck in 1964 and his grandfather won gold at the Lake Placid Games in 1932.

Another contender for Team USA is Chris Soule who won silver at the '00 Winter Goodwill Games. When he's not careening down the ice at Utah Olympic Park, Soule is an actor and stuntman who has had parts in *GI Jane*, *Stepmom*, and *Sex And The City*.

Look for Team USA's Tricia Stumpf, Babs Isak and Lee Ann Parsley to finish in the top ten at the inaugural women's event. Stumpf took home bronze at the 2001 Skeleton World Championships in

# SKI JUMPING

Ski Jumping is one of the original Nordic sports, having been in the Olympics since the beginning. Norway has taken off with 24 total Olympic medals, the most in this sport. Finland has the record for winning the most gold medals with 10. Since 1976, 52 of 54 Olympic medals have gone to Finland, Austria, Japan, Norway, Germany and the Czech Republic.

Ski Jumping has three events, based on the size of the hill. In the Individual normal hill, jumpers launch from a 90 meter-high hill. In Individual large hill, jumpers soar from a 120-meter hill. Each jumper in both of these events takes two jumps and the one with the greatest total score wins.

The crouching form used in the inrun helps jumpers build up speed to push off and soar the farthest.

Alan Alborn is Team USA's best chance for a medal at the 2002 Olympic Winter Games.

Matthew Stockman/Allsport

In the Team large hill event, each member of a four-person team takes two jumps off the 120-meter hill. The inrun, takeoff, flight, landing, and outrun are all watched carefully. Five judges, situated on the side of the hill, carefully observe the jumper's form and landing to determine the style points. The judges use a formula for distance points, and add that to the style points to determine a jumper's point total.

"It's such a rush when you hit that takeoff," said four-time U.S. Jumping champion and two-time Olympian Randy Weber, who retired after the '98 season. "You're going almost 60 miles an hour and then you're in the air. You're only 10 or 12 feet off the ground but, especially as you come over the knoll of the hill and start dropping, it can seem like you've been dropped out of an airplane."

Finland will no doubt be tough to beat since winning their second straight World Cup team title in March of 2001 in Slovenia. Also look for Polish superstar Adam Malysz to bring home Poland's second medal ever in this sport.

Although a podium finish is not expected for Team USA, youngster Alan Alborn is one to watch since becoming the first American to jump over 200 meters. Alborn (also known as "Airborn") enjoys all forms of flying – he has his pilot's license and owns his own single-engine plane. Alborn "flew" for the U.S. Team at the '98 Nagano Games when he qualified for the team at 17-years-old and had the U.S. Team's second best results.

Look for ski jumpers from all over the world flying through the air at Utah Olympic Park in 2002.

Left: This photo shows the starting area where ski jumpers wait for the perfect wind conditions before beginning their jump.

Allsport

Below: A high-angle view of the ski jump event at the 1932 Lake Placid Olympic Winter Games.

Hulton/Allsport

# SNOWBOARDING

Ross Rebagliati of Canada makes a turn in the men's Giant Slalom Snowboarding event at the '98 Nagano Olympic Winter Games. Rebagliati will defend his gold medal in this event in 2002.

Shaun Botterill/Allsport

The sport of Snowboarding was developed during the 1960s in America and reflects that generation's quest to find something new and exciting. That is exactly what Michigander Sherman Poppen was doing in 1965 – Poppen tied two skis together for his daughter and made the first "snurfer." Jake Burton Carpenter took the idea one step further when he opened a small shop in Vermont and started making what is used as today's snowboard.

Snowboarding's Olympic debut occurred in Nagano in 1998. The two Olympic Snowboarding events have only changed slightly – the Alpine event of Giant Slalom has changed to Parallel Giant Slalom. This revised event positions competitors against each other on side-by-side courses. After the first run, the competitors switch courses and go down again. Whoever has the best time wins.

The Half-Pipe is much like the Half-Pipe in skateboarding in that aerial tricks are performed in what looks like a long U-shaped tube. The tube measures 110 meters long and three to four meters deep. This freestyle event is judged for amplitude (how high the snowboarder gets off the lip of the pipe), rotations (tricks with spins), standard maneuvers (tricks without spins), and the overall impression.

At the inaugural Snowboard events at Nagano, Team USA took home bronze medals in both the men's and women's Half-Pipe.

Tricia Byrnes looks like the U.S.'s best chance for a medal in the Half-Pipe. Byrnes finished the 2001 season placed second in World Cup Half-Pipe standings and won gold at the inaugural Winter Goodwill Games in 2000.

Younger teammate Tommy Czeschin has already secured a spot on Team USA, but is still doing everything he can to be in top form for 2002. Czeschin finished sixth in 2001 World Cup standings and won silver at the Goodwill Games.

Alpine Snowboard veteran Sondra Van Ert hopes to lead teammates Anton Pogue and Rosey Fletcher to podium finishes in Park City. Olympian Van Ert, a 37-year-old from Idaho, had two World Cup wins in 2000 and four podium finishes. Pogue finished third at the World Championships and Fletcher won silver at the January 2001 World Cup event.

Team USA's strongest competition will be from France's Karine Ruby, who has won more World Cup races than any other Snowboarder, and Half-Pipe gold medallist Gian Simmen from Switzerland. Simmen won gold with a score of 85.2.

One of the most interesting competition aspects for the 2002 Olympic Winter Games will be how the Alpine snowboarders can adapt to the new Parallel Giant Slalom format. For spectators, it will be one of the most exciting events of all.

Tricia Byrnes hopes to lead her U.S. teammates to the podium in 2002.

Gian Simmen is the man to beat in the Snowboard Halfpipe event after winning gold in Nagano.

NAGANO 1998

# SPEED SKATING – LONG-TRACK

Jonathan Daniel/Allsport

Bonnie Blair won more individual medals (6) than any other U.S. woman.

by making the first all-steel skate.

Speed skates advanced even further with the use of the clap skate at the 1998 Nagano Winter Games. This type of skate has a hinged section where the toe of the boot meets up with the skate. When skating, the heel of the boot comes off the skate, letting the skate remain on the ice for added speed and pushing power.

The men and women have three distance events in common: the 500m, 1000m, and 1500m. The men also have a 5000m and a 10,000m. The women have shorter long-distance events, the 3000m and the 5000m.

Team USA's Olympic Speed Skating history is rich with medals wins. American Charles Jewtraw won the very first gold medal awarded at the inaugural Chamonix Winter Games in 1924. Eric Heiden, then a 21-year-old from Wisconsin, stepped onto the ice in 1980 and took home every single gold medal in the five men's events. Heiden, now an orthopedic surgeon who specializes in sports medicine, recently volunteered to be the Speed Skating team physician for the 2002 Winter Games. He remains the only five-time gold medallist in individual events at a single Olympic Games.

Although no one really knows where skating originated, we do know it has been used for centuries as a mode of transportation in Northern Europe. Skates have been made from everything from bones of elk, deer, reindeer, and horse, to highly waxed wood.

The first metal runner is dated to around 1400 in Holland and it made skating as a means of transport much easier. The first all-iron skate was developed in Scotland in 1572 and Speed Skating as a sport evolved even more. In 1850, a Philadelphia man named E.W. Bushnell took the sport one step further

Five out of nine world records were broken during the March 2001 Speed Skating World Championships at the Utah Olympic Oval.          Todd Warshaw/Allsport

Team USA's Derek Parra was a three-time National Champion and two-time overall World Champion in-line skater before switching to the ice in 1996 in hopes of winning Olympic gold.

Tom Hauck/Allsport

Bonnie Blair is another unforgettable American name in Speed Skating. Blair won more individual medals (6) than any other U.S. woman, in summer or winter competition. Blair won gold in '88 in Calgary, '92 in Albertville, and '94 in Lillehammer and led the way for winning women such as Chris Witty.

Witty is only the ninth American to compete in both the Summer and Winter Olympic Games. Winning bronze in the 1500m and silver in the 1000m the winter before, Witty competed in Cycling at the 2000 Sydney Olympic Games. She recently placed second in the 2000-2001 World Cup standings in the 1000m, behind German Monique Garbrecht-Enfeldt who is also second in the 500m. Also, the U.S. Team's Jennifer Rodriguez should contend for a medal in the 1500m after finishing fourth in that event in World Cup standings.

The German trio of Anni Friesinger, Gunda Niemann-Stirnemann and Claudia Pechstein look to dominate the ladies Long-Track distance events, taking the top three World Cup spots in the 1500m, 3000m and 5000m.

Canadians Jeremy Witherspoon and Michael Ireland are expected to battle Japanese and Norwegian foes for the 500m and 1000m titles. The Dutch men, including returning Olympian Gianni Romme, look to win gold in three out of five of the Long-Track distance events.

The U.S. men should not be counted out, though. Derek Parra, who currently lives in Park City, holds the fifth place spot in the 2000-2001 World Cup standings in the 1500m and won silver in the same event at the 2001 World Single Distance Championships. Teammate Casey FitzRandolph, seventh in both the 500m and 1000m, has the advantage of knowing Olympic action when he competed in Nagano and could medal in one or both of these events. Look for Witty, Parra and FitzRandolph to work even harder on their home ice in 2002.

# SPEED SKATING – SHORT-TRACK

This photo taken at the 2000 Short-Track Speed Skating World Cup at the Peaks Ice Arena in Provo demonstrates how fast skaters take off at the beginning of a race.

Donald Miralle/Allsport

Short-Track Speed Skating developed around the same time Speed Skating became an international sport. But North America did not catch on to the fast-paced, strategic short-track style until the early 1900s. Short-Track debuted at the 1992 Winter Games in Albertville. American Cathy Turner was awarded the first gold medal given at Albertville when she won the 500m event. Turner returned in 1994 and won gold again in the 500m in Lillehammer.

Men and women both have races in the 500m, 1000m, and 1500m distances. The men's Relay is 5000m (45 laps) and the women's is 3000m (27 laps). The men's and women's 1500m event will be making its debut at the 2002 Winter Games.

Because Short-Track events take place on a track the size of a hockey rink, races can be fast, frenzied and dangerous. The walls around the rink are padded to minimize injuries, and contact rules are strictly enforced.

Packs of four to six skaters race against each other and the winner is determined by who finishes first. The Relay races are carefully executed since all of the members of the Relay team remain on the ice during the entire event. Team members usually pass off in the Relay by giving their teammate a push-off from behind, transferring the momentum smoothly.

Team USA has done well in Short-Track Speed Skating in its brief Olympic history. Besides Turner's wins in '92 and '94, the men's and women's Relay team have done well. The men won silver in '94 and the women won silver in '92 and bronze in '94. This season's 5000m Relay team also won a gold medal at the 2001 World Short-Track Championships and stand a good chance of winning gold in 2002.

Amy Peterson, who will be returning to the Winter Games in 2002, won bronze in the 500m, and bronze and silver on the Relay teams in 1994.

Four-time Olympian Peterson holds American records in all four distances.

Peterson will be watching out for China's two Yangs: Yang Yang (A) who won the overall World Cup title, and Yang Yang (S) who placed in the top five in the three World Cup events.

In a sport that has long since been dominated by skaters from Korea, China and Japan, an American powerhouse has emerged. Apolo Anton Ohno, a 19-year-old from Seattle, won the overall World Cup title for the 2000-2001 season after gaining first place in all three distance categories. He is the youngest American to win a World Cup.

Ohno is backed up by teammate Daniel Weinstein, who placed fourth overall at the 2000 World Short-Track Championships and third in the 1000m World Cup final standings.

Weinstein will be able to give advice to his young teammate, since Ohno was only 17 at his first Olympic experience in '98. Look for Ohno to blow by the competition at the Salt Lake Ice Center in 2002.

The judges watch closely as two men tangle at the '94 Lillehammer Games.

Below: Apolo Anton Ohno of the U.S. team hopes to win gold at the 2002 Olympic Winter Games after winning the 2000-2001 overall World Cup title.

## February 11, 2002 – Monday

|  |  |
|---|---|
| 9:00-12:00 | Curling, M Pre. Draw 1, Ice Sheet |
| 9:00-12:30 | Luge, M Singles, Runs 3 & 4 F, UOP |
| 10:00-11:30 | Downhill, W, SSR |
| 10:00-14:00 | Snowboard, M Halfpipe Q & F, PCMR |
| 11:00-15:30 | Biathlon, W 15 km Indiv., SH |
| 11:00-15:30 | Biathlon, M 20 km Indiv., SH |
| 11:00-13:30 | Hockey, W Pre: CAN vs. KAZ, E Center |
| 13:00-14:30 | Speed Skating, M 500m, UOO |
| 14:00-16:30 | Hockey, W Pre: SWE vs. RUS, Peaks |
| 14:00-17:00 | Curling, W Pre. Draw 1, Ice Sheet |
| 16:00-18:30 | Hockey, M Pre: UKR vs. SUI, E Center |
| 17:45-21:30 | Figure Skating, Pairs Free, SLIC |
| 19:00-21:30 | Hockey, M Pre: BLR vs. FRA, Peaks |
| 19:00-22:00 | Curling, M Pre. Draw 2, Ice Sheet |

## February 12, 2002 – Tuesday

|  |  |
|---|---|
| 8:30-11:00 | Ski Jump, M K120 Indiv. Q, UOP |
| 9:00-12:00 | Curling, W Pre. Draw 2, Ice Sheet |
| 9:00-13:00 | Free. Moguls, M Q & F, DV |
| 9:00-13:30 | Cross-Country, W 10 km Classical, SH |
| 9:00-13:30 | Cross-Country, M 15 km Classical, SH |
| 11:00-13:30 | Hockey, W Pre: USA vs. GER, E Center |
| 13:00-14:30 | Speed Skating, M 500m, UOO |
| 14:00-16:30 | Hockey, W Pre: FIN vs. CHN, Peaks |
| 14:00-17:00 | Curling, M Pre. Draw 3, Ice Sheet |
| 16:00-18:30 | Hockey, M Pre: SVK vs. AUT, E Center |
| 16:00-19:00 | Luge, W Singles, Runs 1 & 2, UOP |
| 17:15-21:30 | Figure Skating, M Short Program, SLIC |
| 19:00-21:30 | Hockey, M Pre: GER vs. LAT, Peaks |
| 19:00-22:00 | Curling, W Pre. Draw 3, Ice Sheet |

## February 13, 2002 – Wednesday

|  |  |
|---|---|
| 8:30-11:00 | Ski Jump, M K120 Indiv. F, UOP |
| 9:00-12:00 | Curling, M Pre. Draw 4, Ice Sheet |
| 10:00-15:30 | Comb. Downhill & Slalom, M F, SSA |
| 11:00-13:30 | Hockey, W Pre: RUS vs. CAN, E Center |
| 11:00-15:00 | Biathlon, W 7.5 km Sprint, SH |
| 11:00-15:00 | Biathlon, M 10 km Sprint, SH |
| 14:00-16:30 | Hockey, W Pre: SWE vs. KAZ, Peaks |
| 14:00-17:00 | Curling, W Pre. Draw 4, Ice Sheet |
| 16:00-18:30 | Hockey, M Pre: SUI vs. BLR, E Center |
| 16:00-19:00 | Luge, W Singles, Runs 3 & 4 F, UOP |
| 17:00-18:30 | Speed Skating, W 500m, UOO |
| 18:00-21:30 | ST Speed Skating, W 1500m F, SLIC |
| 18:00-21:30 | ST Speed Skating, M 1000m Pre., SLIC |
| 18:00-21:30 | ST Speed Skating, M 5000m Relay Pre., SLIC |
| 19:00-21:30 | Hockey, M Pre: FRA vs. UKR, Peaks |
| 19:00-22:00 | Curling, M Pre. Draw 5, Ice Sheet |

## February 14, 2002 – Thursday

|  |  |
|---|---|
| 8:30-11:30 | Nordic Comb., M K90 Team F, UOP |
| 9:00-12:00 | Curling, W Pre. Draw 5, Ice Sheet |
| 9:00-12:45 | Cross-Country, M Comb. Pursuit, SH |
| 10:00-14:00 | Snowboard, W Parallel GS Q, PCMR |
| 10:00-14:00 | Snowboard, M Parallel GS Q, PCMR |
| 10:00-15:30 | Comb. Downhill/Slalom, W F, SSA |
| 11:00-13:30 | Hockey, W Pre: FIN vs. GER, Peaks |
| 13:00-14:00 | Comb. Downhill/Slalom, W, SSA |
| 14:00-17:00 | Curling, M Pre. Draw 6, Ice Sheet |
| 15:00-15:30 | Comb. Downhill/Slalom, W, SSA |
| 15:00-17:30 | Hockey, M Class.: A3 vs. B3, E Center |
| 16:00-18:30 | Hockey, W Pre: CHN vs. USA, Peaks |
| 17:00-18:30 | Speed Skating, W 500m, UOO |
| 17:45-22:00 | Figure Skating, M Free, SLIC |
| 19:00-22:00 | Curling, W Pre. Draw 6, Ice Sheet |
| 20:00-22:30 | Hockey, M Class: A2 vs. B2, E Center |
| 21:00-23:30 | Hockey, M Class: A4 vs. B4, Peaks |

## February 15, 2002 – Friday

|  |  |
|---|---|
| 9:00-11:30 | Luge, Doubles F, UOP |
| 9:00-12:00 | Curling, M Pre. Draw 7, Ice Sheet |
| 9:00-14:00 | Cross-Country, W Comb. Pursuit, SH |
| 10:00-12:00 | Snowboard, W Parallel GS F, PCMR |
| 10:00-12:00 | Snowboard, M Parallel GS F, PCMR |
| 11:00-13:30 | Hockey, M F: RUS vs. Qualifier 1, E Center |
| 13:30-14:30 | Nordic Comb., M 4x5 km Team, SH |
| 14:00-16:30 | Hockey, W Pre: KAZ vs. RUS, Peaks |
| 14:00-17:00 | Curling, W Pre. Draw 7, Ice Sheet |
| 15:45-21:00 | Figure Skating, Dance Compulsory, SLIC |
| 16:00-18:30 | Hockey, M F: CAN vs. SWE, E Center |
| 19:00-21:30 | Hockey, M F: CZE vs. Qualifier 2, Peaks |
| 19:00-22:00 | Curling, M Pre. Draw 8, Ice Sheet |
| 20:45-23:15 | Hockey, M F: FIN vs. USA, E Center |

## February 8, 2002 – Friday

# Salt Lake 2002 Olympic Schedule

(times are subject to change)

|  |  |
|---|---|
| 9:00 - 11:30 | Ski Jump, K-90 Indiv. Q, UOP |
| 18:00 - 21:00 | Opening Ceremony, Rice-Eccles |

## February 9, 2002 – Saturday

|  |  |
|---|---|
| 9:00-12:15 | Nordic Combined, K90 Indiv., UOP |
| 9:00-14:00 | Cross-Country, W 15 km Free, SH |
| 9:00-14:00 | Cross-Country, M 30 km Free, SH |
| 9:00-13:00 | Free. Moguls, W Q & F, DV |
| 12:00-15:30 | Speed Skating, M 5000m, UOO |
| 14:00-16:30 | Hockey, M Pre: BLR vs. UKR, Peaks |
| 16:00-18:30 | Hockey, M Pre: SVK vs. GER, E Center |
| 18:30-21:30 | Figure Skating, Pairs Short, SLIC |
| 19:00-21:30 | Hockey, M Pre: AUT vs. LAT, Peaks |
| 21:00-23:30 | Hockey, M Pre: SUI vs. FRA, E Center |

## February 10, 2002 – Sunday

|  |  |
|---|---|
| 8:30-11:00 | Ski Jump, K90 Indiv. F, UOP |
| 9:30-10:30 | Nordic Comb., 15 km Indiv., SH |
| 10:00-11:30 | Downhill, M, SSA |
| 10:00-14:30 | Snowboard, W Halfpipe Q & F, PCMR |
| 13:00-15:30 | Speed Skating, W 3000m, UOO |
| 16:00-18:30 | Hockey, M Pre: AUT vs. GER, Peaks |
| 16:00-19:00 | Luge, M Singles, Runs 1 & 2, UOP |
| 19:00-21:30 | Hockey, M Pre: LAT vs. SVK, E Center |

## February 21, 2002 – Thursday

| | |
|---|---|
| 9:00-12:00 | Curling, W Bronze, Ice Sheet |
| 10:00-14:00 | GS, M F, PCMR |
| 10:30-12:30 | Nordic Comb., M K120 Sprint, Jump portion, UOP |
| 12:00-14:30 | Hockey, W Bronze, Peaks |
| 12:30-14:00 | Cross-Country, W 4x5 km Relay, SH |
| 14:00-17:00 | Curling, W Gold, Ice Sheet |
| 17:00-19:30 | Hockey, W Gold, E Center |
| 17:45-22:00 | Figure Skating, Ladies' Free Program, SLIC |

## February 22, 2002 – Friday

| | |
|---|---|
| 9:00-12:00 | Curling, M Bronze, Ice Sheet |
| 10:00-11:30 | Nordic Comb., 7.5 km Sprint, SH |
| 10:00-14:15 | GS, W F, PCMR |
| 12:00-14:30 | Hockey, M Semifinal: Game 32, E Center |
| 12:00-15:15 | Speed Skating, M 1000m, UOO |
| 13:00-14:00 | GS, W, PCMR |
| 14:30-17:30 | Curling, M Gold, Ice Sheet |
| 14:30-18:45 | Bobsleigh, M 4-Man, Runs 1 & 2, UOP |
| 16:15-18:45 | Hockey, M Semifinal: Game 33, E Center |
| 18:45-21:15 | Figure Skating, Ladies' Exhibition, SLIC |
| 18:45-21:15 | Figure Skating, Men's Exhibition, SLIC |

## February 23, 2002 – Saturday

| | |
|---|---|
| 9:30-13:00 | Cross-Country, M 50 km Classical, SH |
| 10:00-14:00 | Slalom, M F, DVR |
| 12:15-14:45 | Hockey, M Bronze, E Center |
| 13:00-14:45 | Speed Skating, W 5000m, UOO |
| 14:30-18:45 | Bobsleigh, M 4-Man, Runs 3 & 4 F, UOP |
| 18:00-21:00 | ST Speed Skating, W 1000m F, SLIC |
| 18:00-21:00 | ST Speed Skating, M 500m Pre. & F, SLIC |
| 18:00-21:00 | ST Speed Skating, M 5000m Relay F, SLIC |

## February 24, 2002 – Sunday

| | |
|---|---|
| 9:30-12:00 | Cross-Country, W 30km Classical, SH |
| 13:00-15:30 | Hockey, M Gold, E Center |
| 18:00-21:00 | Closing Ceremony, Rice-Eccles |

## February 16, 2002 – Saturday

| | |
|---|---|
| 9:00-12:00 | Curling, W Pre. Draw 8, Ice Sheet |
| 9:00-13:00 | Biathlon, W 10 km Pursuit, SH |
| 9:00-13:00 | Biathlon, M 12.5 km Pursuit, SH |
| 10:00-11:30 | Super-G, M, SSA |
| 10:00-15:00 | Free. Aerials, W Q, DVR |
| 10:00-15:00 | Free. Aerials, M Q, DVR |
| 11:00-13:30 | Hockey, W Pre: USA vs. FIN, E Center |
| 13:00-15:00 | Speed Skating, M 1000m, UOO |
| 14:00-16:30 | Hockey, W Pre: GER vs. CHN, Peaks |
| 14:00-17:00 | Curling, M Pre. Draw 9, Ice Sheet |
| 15:00-18:00 | Bobsleigh, M 2-Man, Runs 1 & 2, UOP |
| 16:45-19:15 | Hockey, M F: FIN vs. Qualifier 1, E Center |
| 18:00-21:00 | ST Speed Skating, W 500m Pre. & F, SLIC |
| 18:00-21:00 | ST Speed Skating, W 3000m Relay Pre., SLIC |
| 18:00-21:00 | ST Speed Skating, M 1000m F, SLIC |
| 19:00-21:30 | Hockey, W Pre: CAN vs. SWE, Peaks |
| 19:00-22:00 | Curling, M Pre. Draw 9, Ice Sheet |
| 21:30-24:00 | Hockey, M F: USA vs. RUS, E Center |

## February 17, 2002 – Sunday

| | |
|---|---|
| 9:00-12:00 | Curling, M Pre. Draw 10, Ice Sheet |
| 9:00-11:00 | Cross-Country, M 4x10 km Relay, SH |
| 10:00-11:30 | Super-G, W, SSA |
| 14:00-16:30 | Hockey, W Class: A3 vs. B4, Peaks |
| 14:00-17:00 | Curling, W Pre. Draw 10, Ice Sheet |
| 15:00-18:30 | Bobsleigh, M 2-Man, Runs 3 & 4 F, UOP |
| 16:00-18:30 | Hockey, M F: SWE vs. CZE, E Center |
| 17:15-19:15 | Speed Skating, W 1000m, UOO |
| 17:30-21:00 | Figure Skating, Dance Original, SLIC |
| 19:00-21:30 | Hockey, M F: CAN vs. Qualifier 2, Peaks |
| 19:00-22:00 | Curling, M Pre. Draw 11, Ice Sheet |
| 21:00-23:30 | Hockey, W Class: B3 vs. A4, E Center |

## February 18, 2002 – Monday

| | |
|---|---|
| 8:30-11:30 | Ski Jump, M K120 Team F, UOP |
| 9:00-12:00 | Curling, W Pre. Draw 11, Ice Sheet |
| 11:00-13:30 | Hockey, M F: Qualifier 1 vs. USA, E Center |
| 11:30-13:30 | Biathlon, W 4x7.5 km Relay, SH |
| 12:00-13:00 | Free. Aerials, W F, DVR |
| 13:30-16:00 | Hockey, M F: RUS vs. FIN, Peaks |
| 14:00-17:00 | Curling, M Pre. Draw 12, Ice Sheet |
| 16:00-18:30 | Hockey, M F: CZE vs. CAN, E Center |
| 17:15-21:15 | Figure Skating, Dance Free, SLIC |
| 19:00-21:30 | Hockey, M F: Qualifier 2 vs. SWE, Peaks |
| 19:00-22:00 | Curling, W Pre. Draw 12, Ice Sheet |

## February 19, 2002 – Tuesday

| | |
|---|---|
| 9:00-14:30 | Cross-Country, M 1.5 km Sprint, SH |
| 9:00-14:30 | Cross-Country, W 1.5 km Sprint, SH |
| 11:00-13:30 | Hockey, W Semifinal: A1 vs. B2, E Center |
| 12:00-13:00 | Free. Aerials, M F, DVR |
| 13:00-15:30 | Speed Skating, M 1500m, UOO |
| 14:00-16:30 | Hockey, W Class: 7th vs. 8th, Peaks |
| 15:30-18:30 | Bobsleigh, 2-Woman F, UOP |
| 16:30-19:00 | Hockey, W Semifinal: B1 vs. A2, E Center |
| 17:15-21:30 | Figure Skating, Ladies Short, SLIC |
| 19:00-21:30 | Hockey, W Class: 5th vs. 6th, Peaks |

## February 20, 2002 – Wednesday

| | |
|---|---|
| 9:00-12:00 | Curling, W Semifinals, Ice Sheet |
| 9:00-12:00 | Skeleton, W Singles, UOP |
| 9:00-12:00 | Skeleton, M Singles, UOP |
| 10:00-14:00 | Slalom, W F, DVR |
| 11:00-13:00 | Biathlon, M 4x7.5 km Relay, SH |
| 13:00-15:00 | Speed Skating, W 1500m, UOO |
| 13:30-15:30 | Hockey, M Quarterfinals: D2 vs. C3, Peaks |
| 13:30-16:00 | Hockey, M Quarterfinal: C1 vs. D4, E Center |
| 14:00-17:00 | Curling, M Semifinals, Ice Sheet |
| 16:00-18:30 | Hockey, M Quarterfinal: C2 vs. D3, E Center |
| 18:00-21:00 | ST Speed Skating, W 1000m Pre., SLIC |
| 18:00-21:00 | ST Speed Skating, W 3000m Relay F, SLIC |
| 18:00-21:00 | ST Speed Skating, M 1500m F, SLIC |
| 20:15-22:45 | Hockey, M Quarterfinal: D1 vs. C4, E Center |